Deck the Hall

Holiday A Cappella Trios

SAB Series

A Cappella Arrangements by
Deke Sharon

Edited by Anne Raugh

EXCLUSIVELY DISTRIBUTED BY

HAL•LEONARD®
CORPORATION

7777 W. BLUEMOUND RD. P.O. BOX 13819 MILWAUKEE, WI 53213

TABLE OF CONTENTS

Cover photo: Kyle Stetson, *Sweet Brats*
© 2004 Mainely A Cappella
Photo: Kate Gooding

Carol of the Bells

Arrangement by
Deke Sharon

Traditional

ding ding-a dong, ding ding-a dong, ding ding-a dong, ding ding-a dong,
ding ding-a dong, ding ding-a dong, ding ding-a dong, ding ding-a dong,
ding dong ding___ dong ding-a ding dong

ding ding-a dong-a ding ding-a dong-a ding ding-a dong-a ding ding-a dong,
ding ding-a dong, ding ding-a dong, ding ding-a dong, ding ding-a dong,
ding ding-a dong-a ding ding-a dong, ding ding-a dong-a ding ding-a dong,

ding-a ding-a ding-a ding-a dong dong ding-a ding-a ding-a ding-a dong dong
ding, ding dong, ding, ding dong,
ding ding-a dong, ding ding-a dong, ding ding-a dong, ding ding-a dong,

ding ding - a dong, ding ding - a dong, ding ding - a dong, ding ding - a ding
ding, ding dong, dong ding, ding dong ding
ding, ding dong, dong ding, ding dong ding

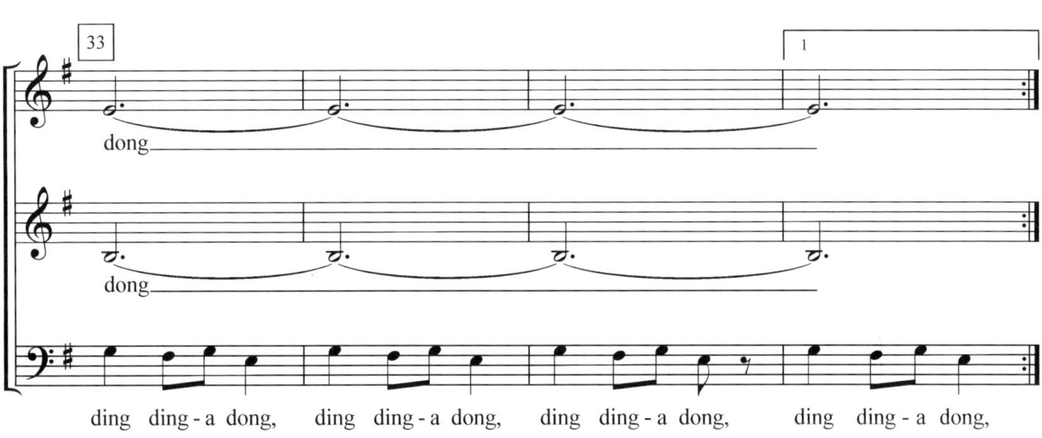

33
1
dong
dong
ding ding - a dong, ding ding - a dong, ding ding - a dong, ding ding - a dong,

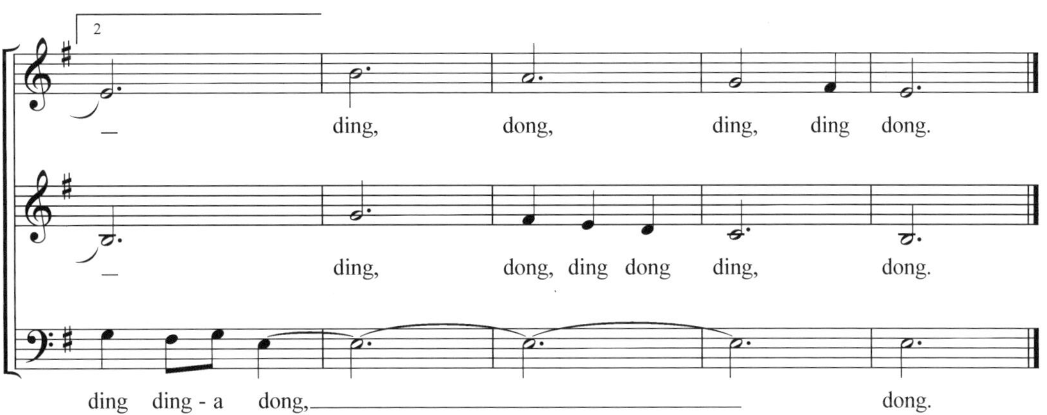

2
ding, dong, ding, ding dong.
ding, dong, ding dong ding, dong.
ding ding - a dong, dong.

Deck the Hall

Arrangement by
Deke Sharon

Traditional Welsh

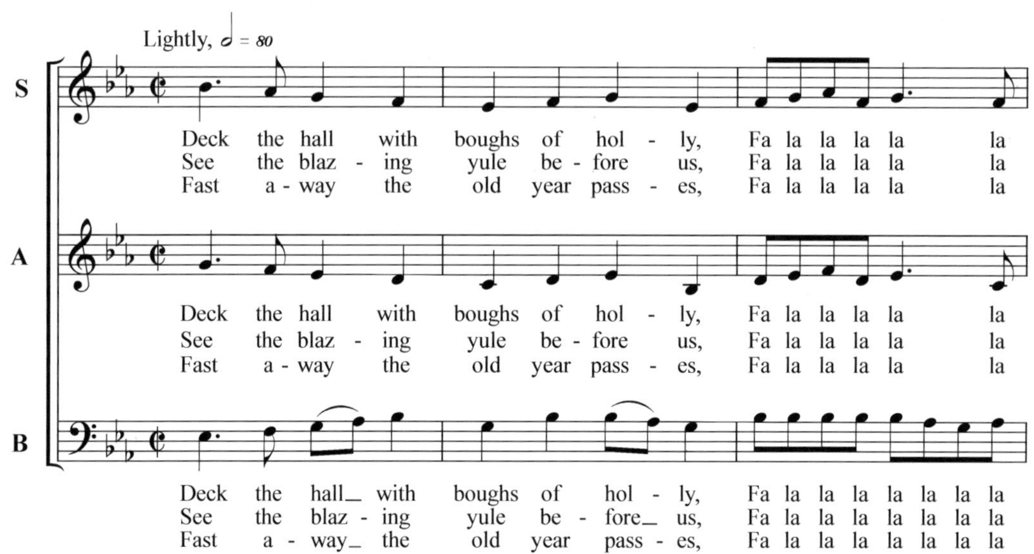

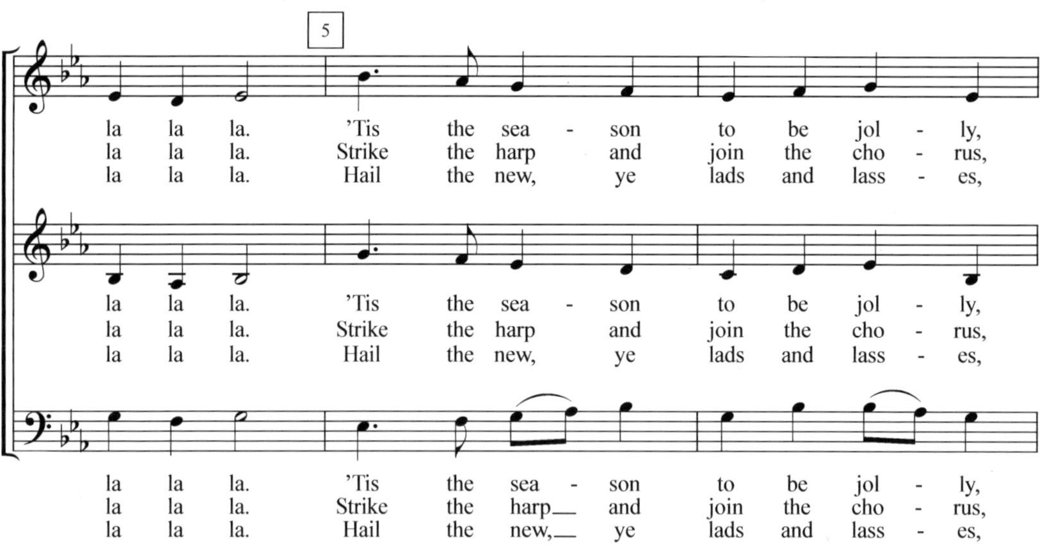

9
Fa la la la la la la la la. Don we now our gay ap-par-el,
Fa la la la la la la la la. Fol-low me in mer-ry mea-sure,
Fa la la la la la la la la. Sing we joy-ous all to-geth-er,

Fa la la la la la la la la. Don we now our gay ap-par-el,
Fa la la la la la la la la. Fol-low me in mer-ry mea-sure,
Fa la la la la la la la la. Sing we joy-ous all to-geth-er,

Fa la la la la la la la la la la. Don we now our gay ap-par-el,
Fa la la la la la la la la la la. Fol-low me in mer-ry mea-sure,
Fa la la la la la la la la la la. Sing we joy-ous all to-geth-er,

13
Fa la la, la la la, la la la. Troll the an-cient
Fa la la, la la la, la la la. While I tell of
Fa la la, la la la, la la la. Heed-less of the

Fa la la la la, fa la la. Troll the an-cient
Fa la la la la, fa la la. While I tell of
Fa la la la la, fa la la. Heed-less of the

Fa la la la la la la la, fa la la la, Troll the an-cient
Fa la la la la la la la, fa la la la, While I tell of
Fa la la la la la la la, fa la la la, Heed-less of the

Yule-tide car-ol, Fa la la la la la la la la.
Yule-tide trea-sure, Fa la la la la la la la la.
wind and weath-er, Fa la la la la la la la la.

Yule-tide car-ol, Fa la la la la la la la la.
Yule-tide trea-sure, Fa la la la la la la la la.
wind and weath-er, Fa la la la la la la la la.

Yule-tide car-ol, Fa la la la, fa la la la la la la la.
Yule-tide trea-sure, Fa la la la, fa la la la la la la la.
wind and weath-er, Fa la la la, fa la la la la la la la.

Good King Wenceslas

Arrangement by
Deke Sharon

Music by Piae Cantiones
Lyrics by J. M. Neale

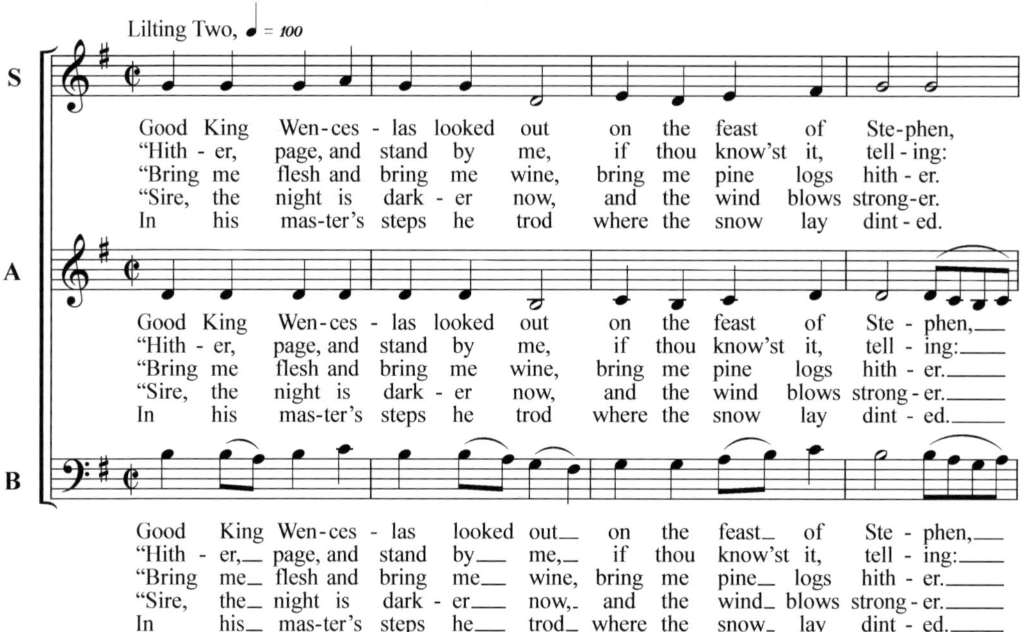

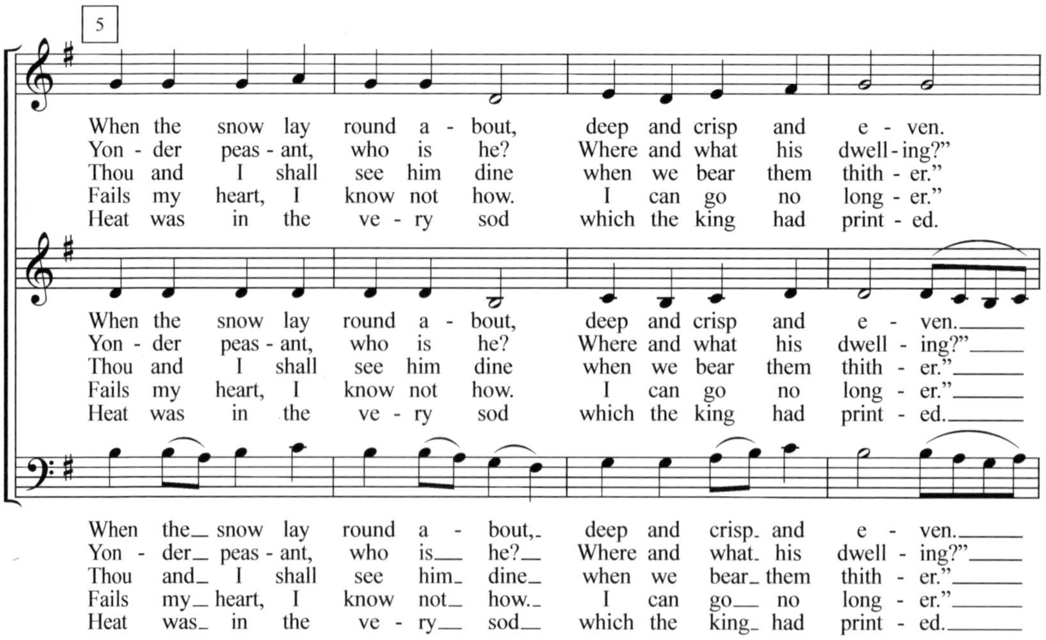

9
Bright - ly shone the moon that night, though the frost was cru - el,
"Sire, he lives a good league hence, un - der - neath the moun - tain,
Page and mon - arch, forth they went, forth they went to - geth - er,
"Mark my foot - steps, good my page, tread thou in them bold - ly.
There - fore all ye men be sure, wealth or rank pos - sess - ing,

Bright - ly shone the moon that night, though the frost was cru - el,____
"Sire, he lives a good league hence, un - der - neath the moun - tain,____
Page and mon - arch, forth they went, forth they went to - geth - er,____
"Mark my foot - steps, good my page, tread thou in them bold - ly.____
There - fore all ye men be sure, wealth or rank pos - sess - ing,____

Bright - ly shone the moon that night, though the frost_ was cru - el,____
"Sire, he lives a good league hence, un - der - neath_ the moun - tain,____
Page and mon - arch, forth they went, forth they went_ to - geth - er,____
"Mark my foot - steps, good my page, tread thou in__ them bold - ly.____
There - fore all ye men be sure, wealth or rank_ pos - sess - ing,____

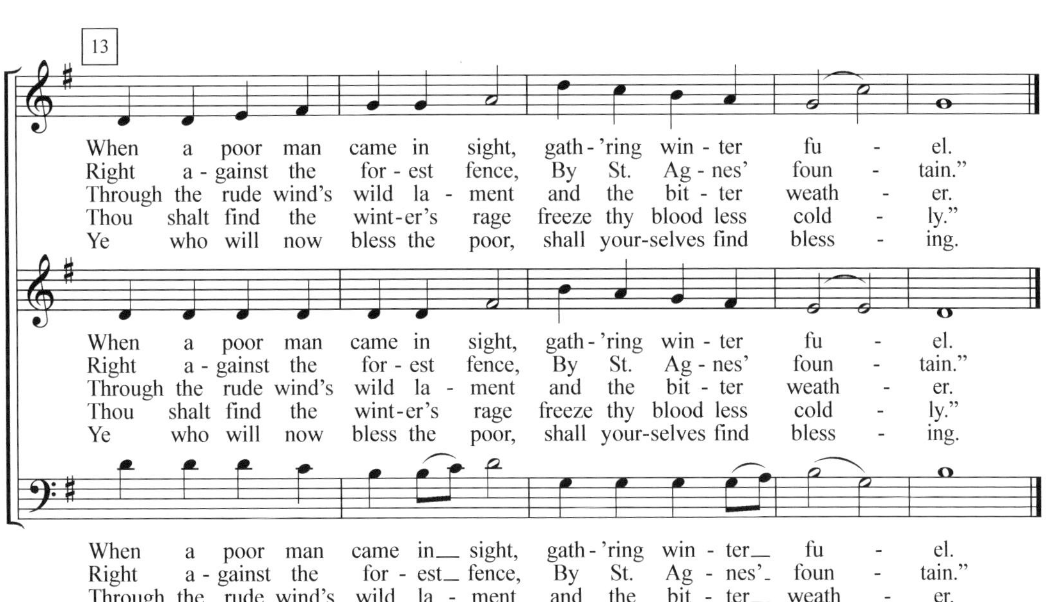
13
When a poor man came in sight, gath - 'ring win - ter fu - el.
Right a - gainst the for - est fence, By St. Ag - nes' foun - tain."
Through the rude wind's wild la - ment and the bit - ter weath - er.
Thou shalt find the wint-er's rage freeze thy blood less cold - ly."
Ye who will now bless the poor, shall your-selves find bless - ing.

When a poor man came in sight, gath - 'ring win - ter fu - el.
Right a - gainst the for - est fence, By St. Ag - nes' foun - tain."
Through the rude wind's wild la - ment and the bit - ter weath - er.
Thou shalt find the wint-er's rage freeze thy blood less cold - ly."
Ye who will now bless the poor, shall your-selves find bless - ing.

When a poor man came in__ sight, gath - 'ring win - ter_ fu - el.
Right a - gainst the for - est_ fence, By St. Ag - nes'_ foun - tain."
Through the rude wind's wild la - ment and the bit - ter_ weath - er.
Thou shalt find the wint - er's_ rage freeze thy blood less_ cold - ly."
Ye who will now bless the_ poor, shall your-selves find_ bless - ing.

The Hanukkah Song

Arrangement by
Deke Sharon

Traditional

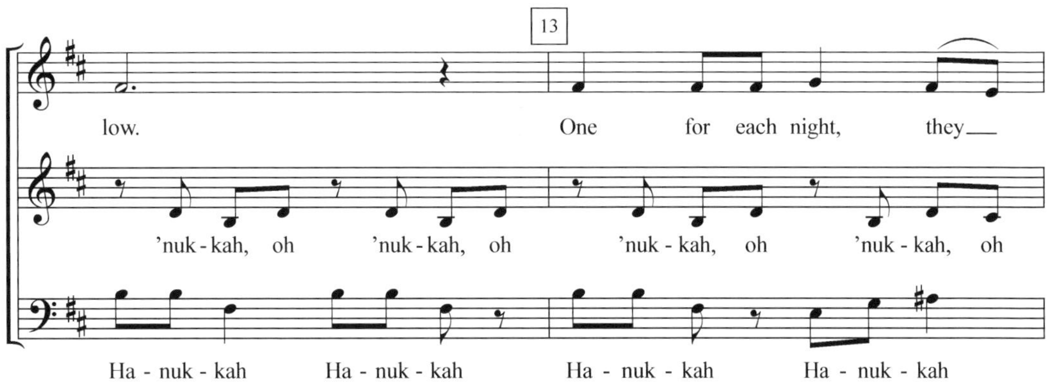
13
low.   One   for each night,   they___
'nuk-kah, oh   'nuk-kah, oh   'nuk-kah, oh   'nuk-kah, oh
Ha - nuk - kah   Ha - nuk - kah   Ha - nuk - kah   Ha - nuk - kah

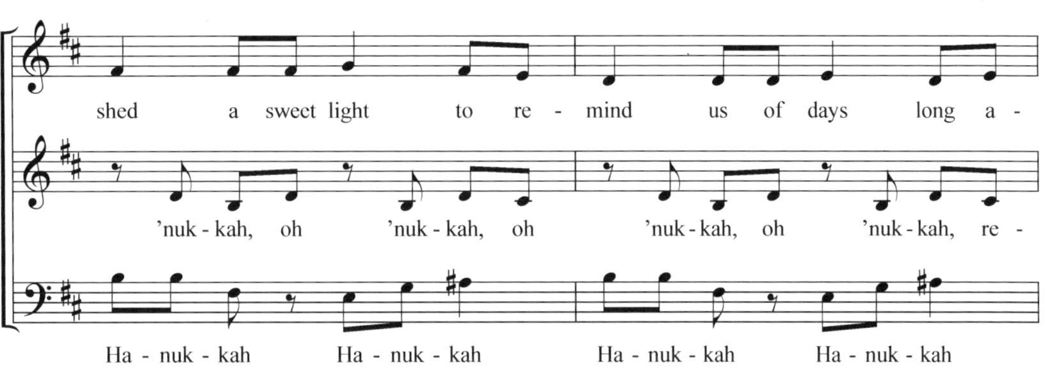
shed   a sweet light   to re - mind   us   of days   long a -
'nuk - kah, oh   'nuk - kah, oh   'nuk - kah, oh   'nuk - kah, re -
Ha - nuk - kah   Ha - nuk - kah   Ha - nuk - kah   Ha - nuk - kah

17
go.___________________   One   for each night, they___
mind   us   of days   long a - go.   for each night,   they___
Ha - nuk - kah   Ha - nuk - kah, oh   One   for each night,   they

shed   a sweet light   to re - mind   us   of days   long a - go.
shed   a sweet light   to re - mind   us   of days   long a - go.
shed   a sweet light   to re - mind   us   of days   long a - go.

Here We Come a-Caroling

Arrangement by
Deke Sharon

Traditional English

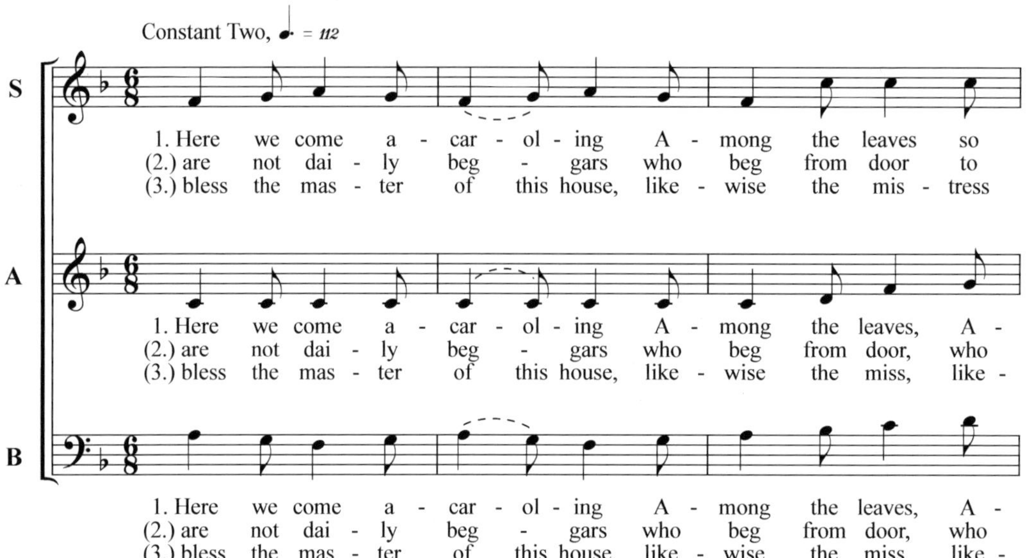

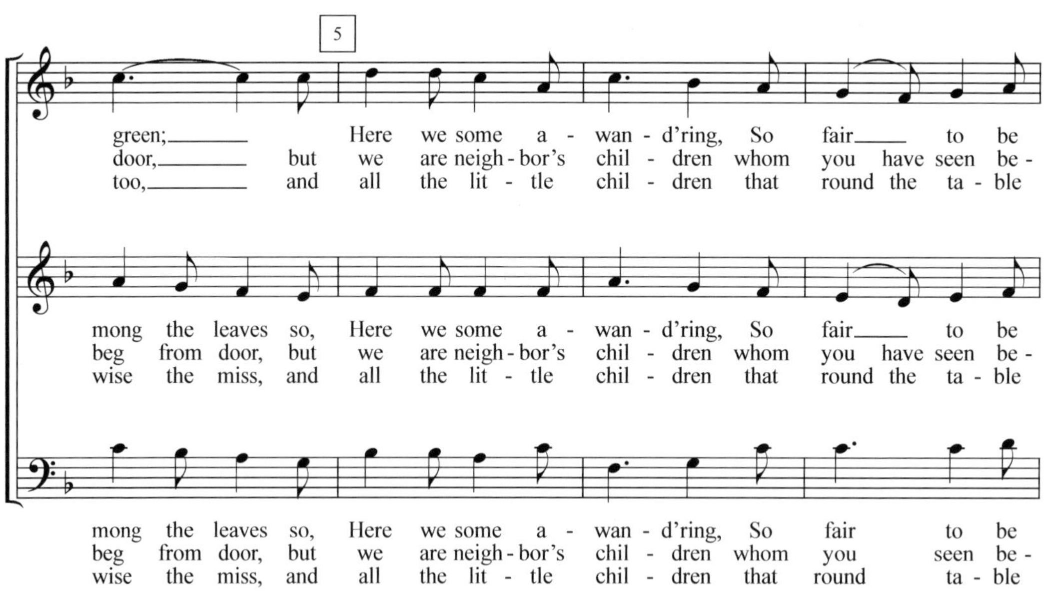

9
Love and joy come to you, And to you glad Christ - mas
seen.
fore.
go.
Love and joy come to you, And to you glad Christ - mas
seen.
fore.
go.
Love and joy come to you, And to you glad Christ - mas
seen.
fore.
go.
13
too; And God bless you and send you a hap - py New
too; And God bless you and send you a hap - py New
too; And God bless you and send you a hap - py New
17
Year, And God send you a Hap - py New Year. 2. We
3. God
Year, And God send you a Hap - py New Year. 2. We
3. God
Year, And God send you a Hap - py New Year. 2. We
3. God

Jingle Bells

Arrangement by
Deke Sharon

Words and Music by
John Pierpont

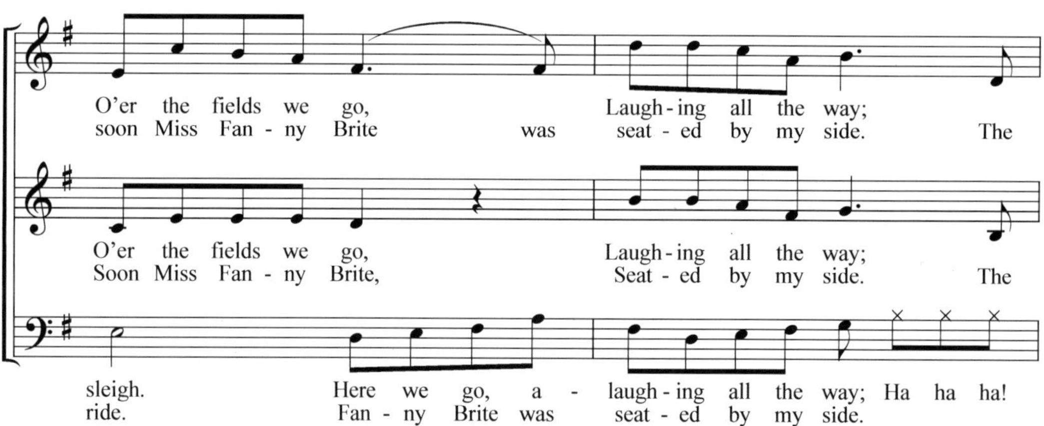

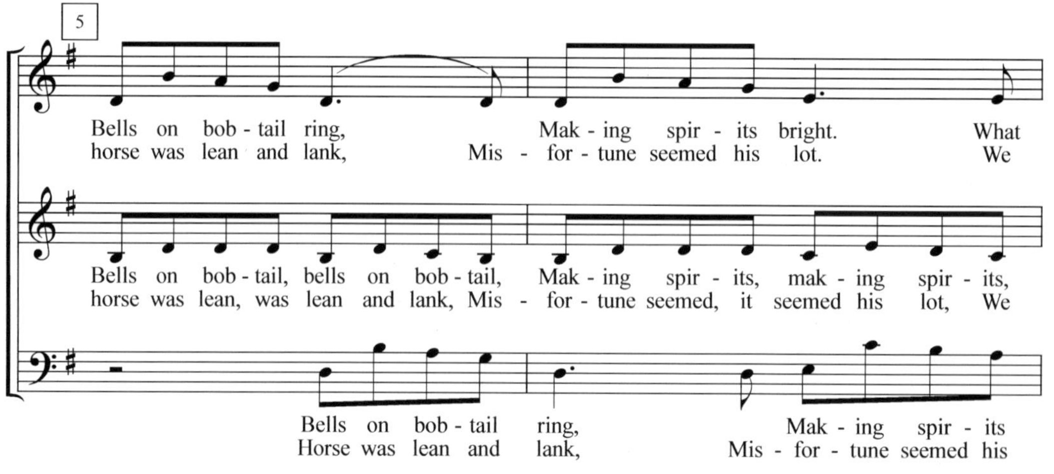

fun it is to ride and sing a sleigh-ing song to-night. Oh,
got in-to a drift-ed bank and then we got up-sot! Oh,
fun it is to ride and sing, sleigh-ing song to-night. Oh,
got in-to a drift-ed bank, then we got up-sot! Oh,
bright, Oh what fun, a sleigh-ing song to-night. Oh,
lot, Drift-ed bank, and then we got up-sot! Oh,
Jin-gle bells, jin-gle bells, jin-gle all the way; Oh what fun it is to ride in a
Jin-gle bells, jin-gle bells, jin-gle all the way; Oh what fun it is to ride in a
Jin-gle, jin-gle, jin-gle, jin-gle, jin-gle, jin-gle, jin-gle, jin-gle, Oh what fun, in a
one-horse o-pen sleigh. Oh, Jin-gle bells, jin-gle bells, jin-gle all the way;
one-horse o-pen sleigh. Oh, Jin-gle bells, jin-gle bells, jin-gle all the way;
one-horse o-pen sleigh. Oh, Jin-gle, jin-gle, jin-gle, jin-gle, jin-gle, jin-gle, jin-gle, jin-gle,
Oh what fun it is to ride in a one-horse o-pen sleigh. Hey! A one-horse o-pen sleigh. Hey!
Oh what fun it is to ride in a one-horse open sleigh. Hey! A one-horse o-pen sleigh. Hey!
Oh what fun it is to ride in a one-horse o-pen sleigh. Hey! one-horse o-pen sleigh. Hey!

Jolly Old Saint Nicholas

Arrangement by
Deke Sharon

Traditional United States

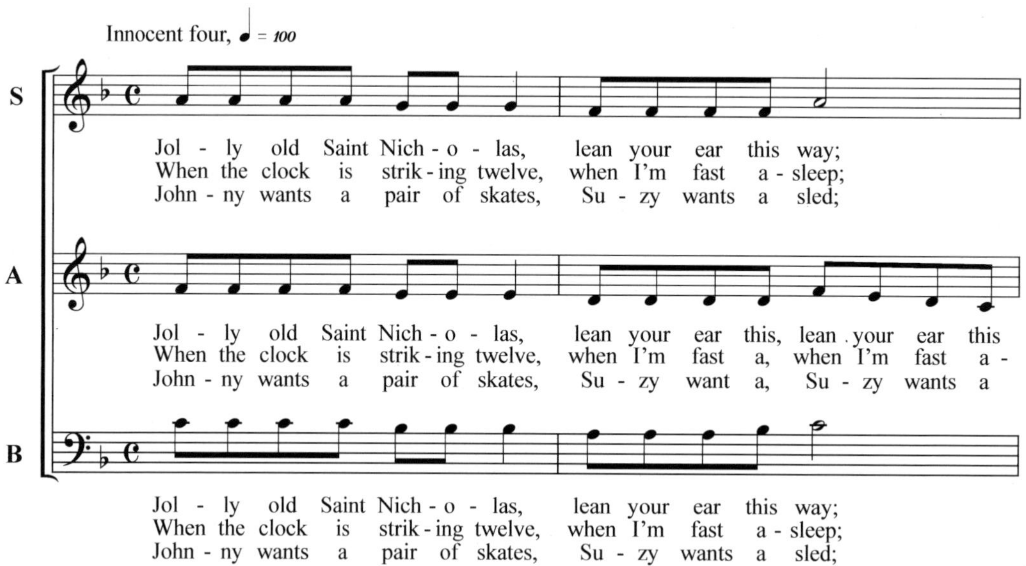

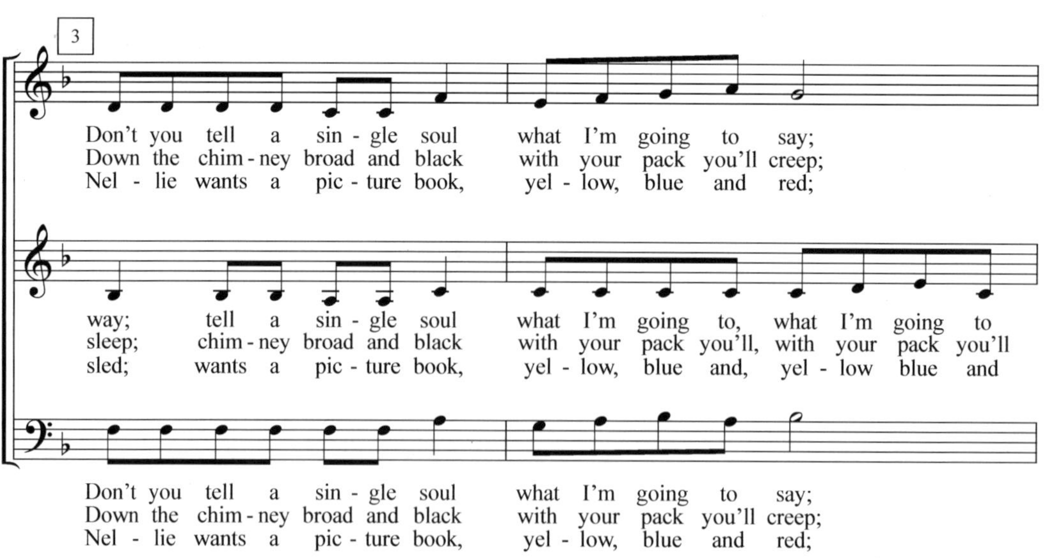

5
Christ - mas Eve is com - ing soon, now, you dear old man;
All the stock - ings you will find hang - ing in a row;
Now I think I'll leave to you what to give the rest;

say; Eve is com - ing soon, now, you dear old, now, you dear old
creep; stock - ings you will find, hang - ing in a, hang - ing in a
red; think I'll leave to you, what to give the, what to give the

Christ - mas Eve is com - ing soon, now, you dear old man;
All the stock - ings you will find hang - ing in a row;
Now I think I'll leave to you what to give the rest;

7
Whis - per what you'll bring to me, tell me if you can.
Mine will be the short - est one, you'll be sure to know.
Choose for me, dear San - ta Claus, you will know the best.

man; what you'll bring to me, tell me if you can.
row; be the short - est one, you'll be sure to know.
rest; me, dear San - ta Claus, you will know the best.

Whis - per what you'll bring to me, tell me if you can.
Mine will be the short - est one, you'll be sure to know.
Choose for me, dear San - ta Claus, you will know the best.

O Christmas Tree

Arrangement by
Deke Sharon

Traditional German

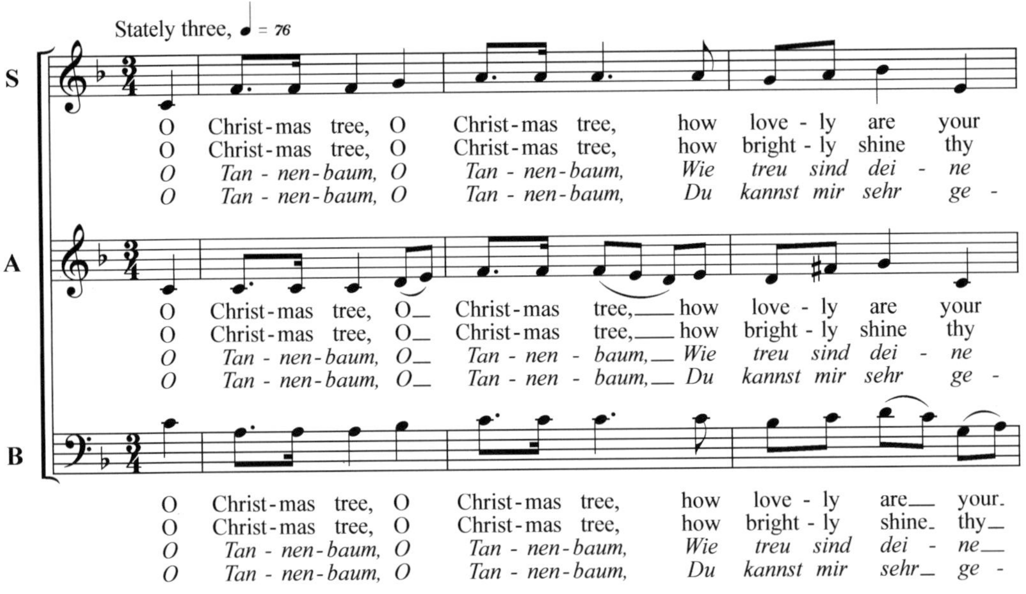

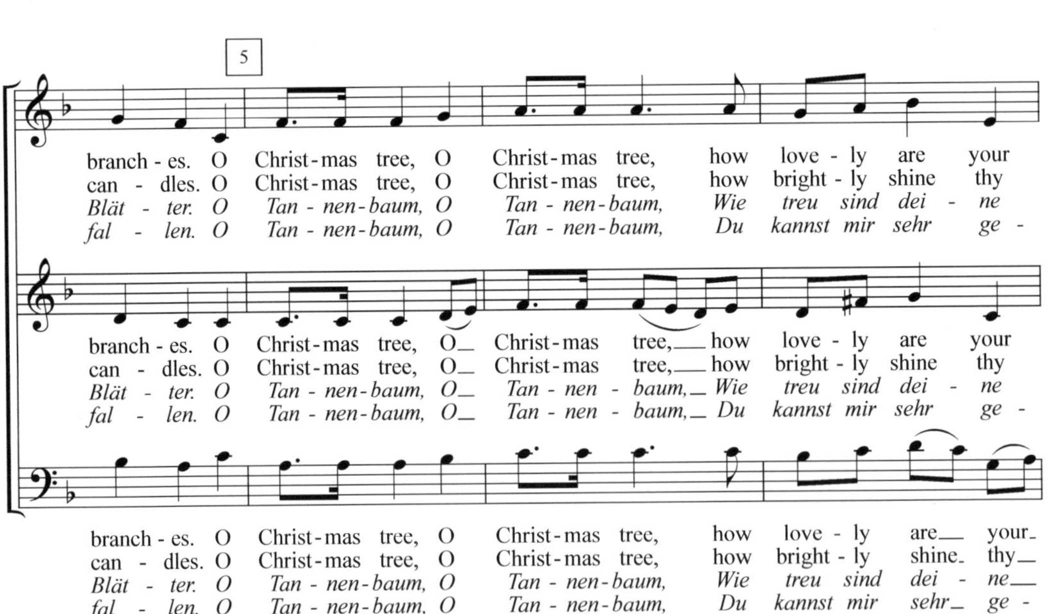

branch - es. Your boughs so green in sum - mer time stay
can - dles. And from each bough a ti - ny light adds
Blät - ter. Du grünst nicht nur zur Som - mers - zeit, Nein,
fal - len. Wie oft hat nicht zur Weih - nachts - zeit, Ein

branch - es. Your boughs so green in sum - mer time stay
can - dles. And from each bough a ti - ny light adds
Blät - ter. Du grünst nicht nur zur Son - mers - zeit, Nein,
fal - len. Wie oft hat night zur Weih - nachts - zeit, Ein

branch - es. Your boughs so green in sum - mer time stay
can - dles. And from each bough a ti - ny light adds
Blät - ter. Du grünst nicht nur zur Som - mers - zeit, Nein,
fal - len. Wie oft hat nicht zur Weih - nachts - zeit, Ein

brave - ly green in win - ter time. O Christ - mas tree, O
to the splen - dor of the sight. O Christ - mas tree, O
auch im Win - ter, wenn es schneit. O Tan - nen - baum, O
Baum von dir mich hoch er - freut. O Tan - nen - baum, O

brave - ly green in win - ter time. O Christ - mas tree, O
to the splen - dor of the sight. O Christ - mas tree, O
auch im Win - ter, wenn es schneit. O Tan - nen - baum, O
Baum von dir mich hoch er - freut. O Tan - nen - baum, O

brave - ly green in win - ter time. O Christ - mas tree, O
to the splen - dor of the sight. O Christ - mas tree, O
auch im Win - ter, wenn es schneit. O Tan - nen - baum, O
Baum von dir mich hoch er - freut. O Tan - nen - baum, O

Christ - mas tree, how love - ly are your branch - es.
Christ - mas tree, how bright - ly shine thy can - dles.
Tan - nen - baum, Wie treu sind dei - ne Blät - ter!
Tan - nen - baum, Du kannst mir sehr ge - fal - len.

Christ - mas tree, how love - ly are your branch - es.
Christ - mas tree, how bright - ly shine thy can - dles.
Tan - nen - baum, Wie treu sind dei - ne Blät - ter!
Tan - nen - baum, Du kannst mir sehr ge - fal - len.

Christ - mas tree, love - ly are your branch - es.
Christ - mas tree, bright - ly shine thy can - dles.
Tan - nen - baum, treu sind dei - ne Blät - ter!
Tan - nen - baum, kannst mir sehr ge - fal - len.

Silent Night

Arrangement by
Deke Sharon

Words and Music by
Franz Xavier Gruber

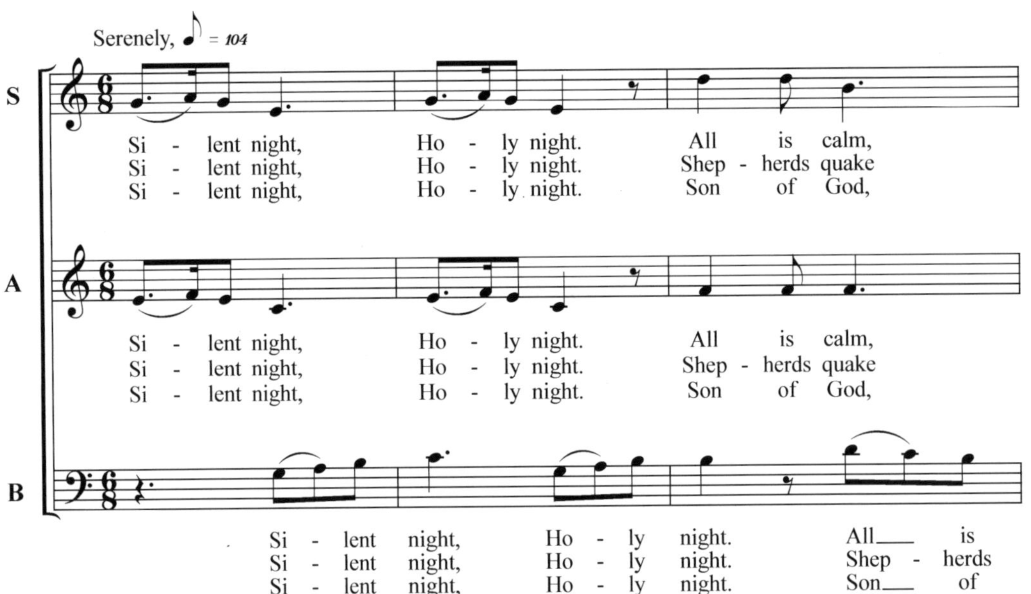

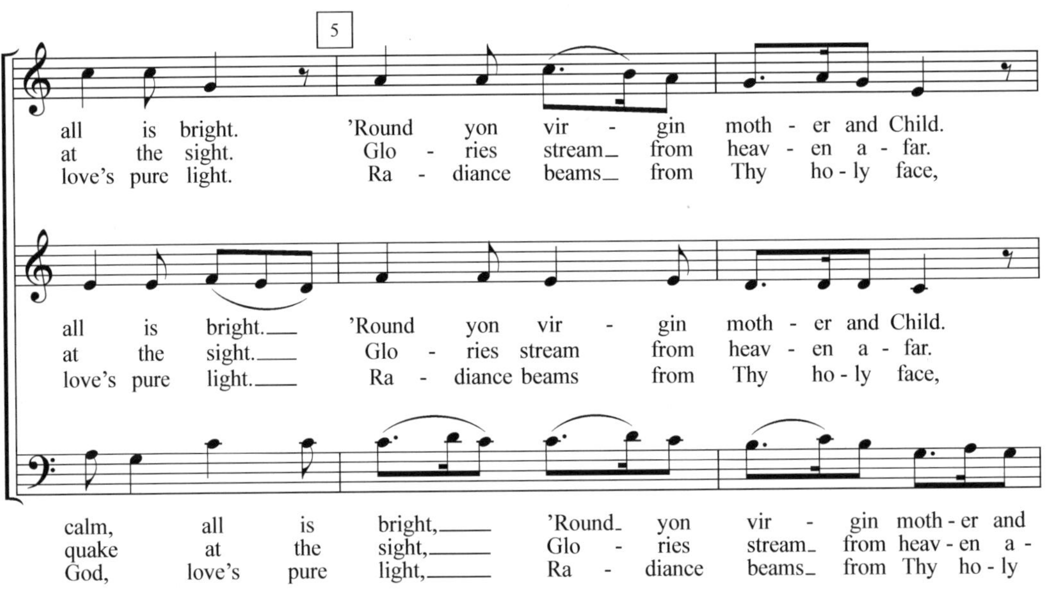

9

Ho - ly In - fant, so ten - der and mild. Sleep in heav - en - ly
Heav - 'nly hosts sing, "Al - le - lu - ia!" Christ, the Sa - viour is
with the dawn of re - deem - ing grace. Je - sus, Lord, at Thy

Moth - er and Child, so ten - der and mild. Sleep in heav - en - ly
Heav - en a - far, sing, "Al - le - lu - ia!" Christ, the Sa - viour is
Thy ho - ly face, re - deem - ing grace. Je - sus, Lord, at Thy

Child, an In - fant, so ten - der and mild. Sleep in heav - en - ly
far, heav - en sing, "Al - le - lu - ia!" Christ, the Sa - viour is
face, the dawn of re - deem - ing grace. Je - sus, Lord, at Thy

peace, Sleep in heav - en - ly peace.
born! Christ, the Sa - viour is born.
birth, Je - sus, Lord, at Thy birth.

peace, in heav - en - ly, Sleep in heav - en - ly peace.
born, the Sa - viour is, Christ, the Sa - viour is born.
birth, Lord, at Thy, Je - sus, Lord, at Thy birth.

peace, in heav - en - ly, Sleep in heav - en - ly peace.
born, the Sa - viour is, Christ, the Sa - viour is born.
birth, Lord, at Thy, Je - sus, Lord, at Thy birth.

Stille Nacht

Arrangement by
Deke Sharon

Words and Music by
Franz Xavier Gruber

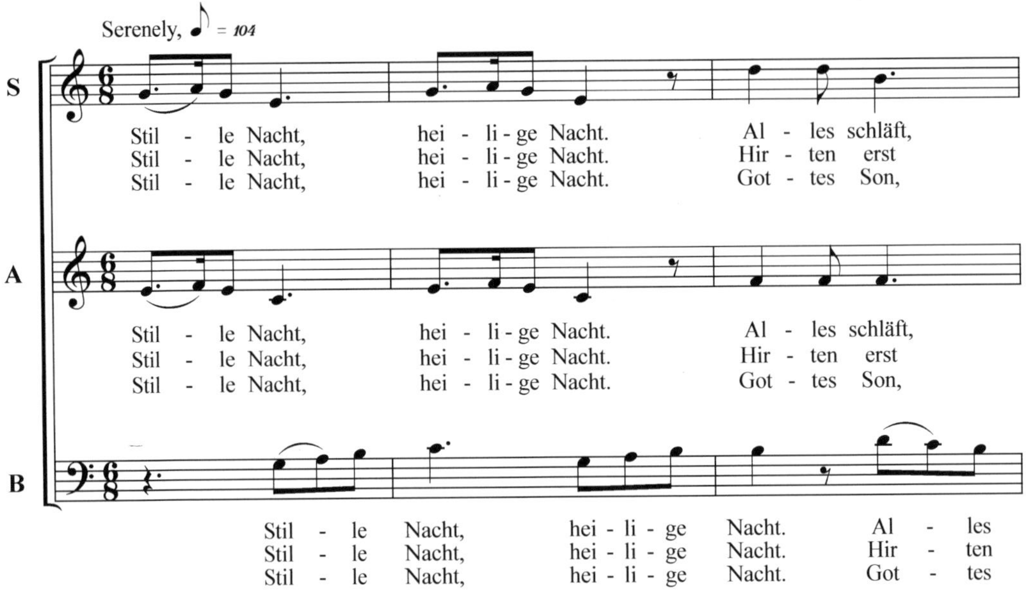

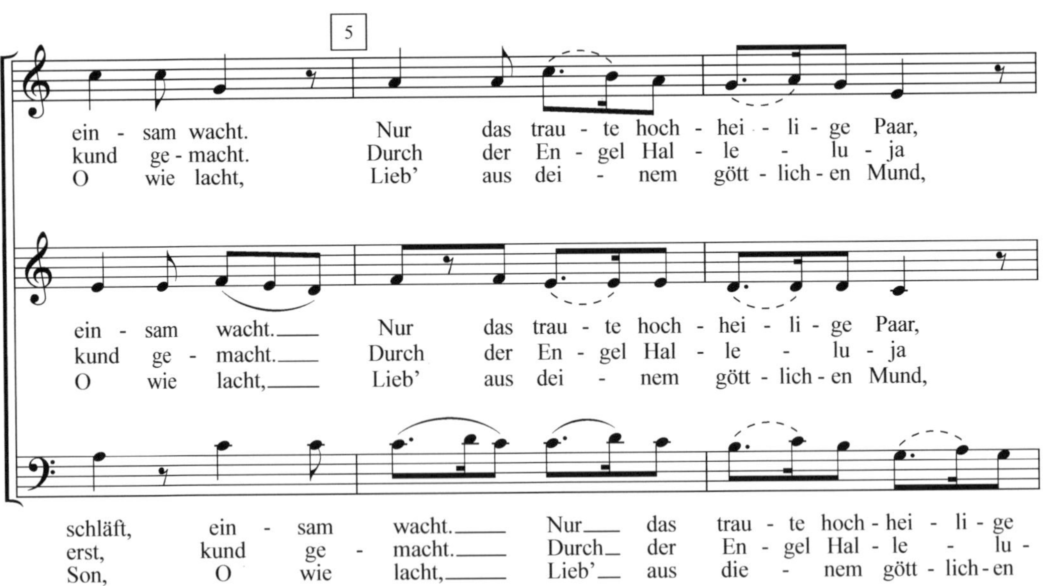

9
Hol - der Kna - be mit lok - ki - gem Haar. Schlaf in himm - li - scher
Tönt es laut von fern und nah: Christ, der Ret - ter, ist
Das uns schlägt die ret - ten - de Stund', Christ in dei - ner Ge -

Hol - der Kna - be mit lok - ki - gem Haar. Schlaf in himm - li - scher
Tönt es laut von fern und nah: Christ, der Ret - ter, ist
Das uns schlägt die ret - ten - de Stund', Christ in dei - ner Ge -

Paar. Kna - be mit lok - ki - gem Haar. Schlaf in himm - li - scher
ja es laut von fern und nah: Christ, der Ret - ter, ist
Mund, uns schlägt die re - ten - de Stund', Christ in dei - ner Ge -

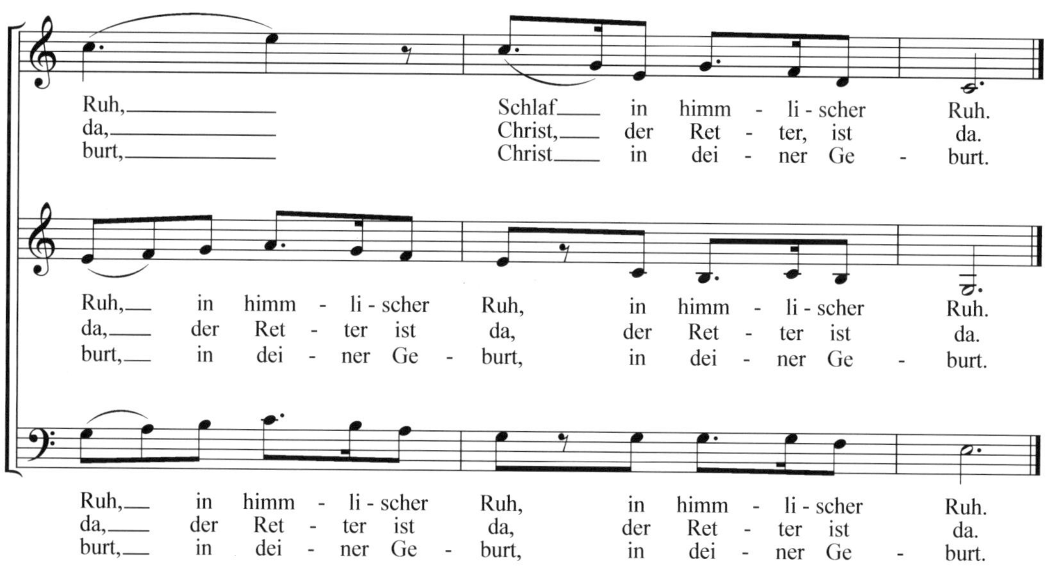
Ruh, Schlaf in himm - li - scher Ruh.
da, Christ, der Ret - ter, ist da.
burt, Christ in dei - ner Ge - burt.

Ruh, in himm - li - scher Ruh, in himm - li - scher Ruh.
da, der Ret - ter ist da, der Ret - ter ist da.
burt, in dei - ner Ge - burt, in dei - ner Ge - burt.

Ruh, in himm - li - scher Ruh, in himm - li - scher Ruh.
da, der Ret - ter ist da, der Ret - ter ist da.
burt, in dei - ner Ge - burt, in dei - ner Ge - burt.

We Wish You a Merry Christmas

9
hap - py new year.)
bring it right here!} Good tid-ings we bring to you and your kin. We
bring it right here!)

hap - py new year.)
bring it right here!} Good tid-ings we bring to you and your kin. We
bring it right here!)

hap - py new_ year.)
bring it right_ here!} Good_ tid-ings we bring_ to_ you and your kin._ We_
bring it right_ here!)

13
wish you a mer - ry Christ - mas and a hap - py new year.

wish you a mer - ry Christ - mas and a hap - py_ new year.

wish you a mer - ry Christ - mas, hap - py_ new_ year.

PERFORMANCE NOTES

Although SAB is a common format, it can span a wide variety of singers with varying vocal ranges, from junior high to adult. It was our intention with this songbook to create arrangements that could be sung by any configuration of SAB voices. However, this does not mean every note is perfect for your ensemble. We encourage you to custom-tailor these arrangements to your liking. Move the overall key up or down, drop baritone notes an octave, change the form, add vocal percussion, etc. In the end, all that matters is how good the arrangement sounds, not how closely it reflects what's on paper.

These arrangements grew from the Sharon family annual holiday party, and work well with an informal, mixed group of singers (I invite men who can't sight-read to sing an octave lower).

Carol of the Bells: To get the best sound, focus less on pronouncing the "ding" and "dong" and more on a resonant, ringing, syllable. If you'd like to sing this with lyrics, several different versions in English can be found online.

Deck the Hall: If singing as a concert piece (as opposed to informal caroling), consider varying the dynamics and tempo in various phrases. You can repeat the last two measures if you'd like to create a more definitive ending.

Good King Wenceslas: If performing with a multi-voice choir, consider using a trio for the lines declared by Wenceslas, a separate trio for the page's lines, and having the entire group sing the narration. If performing at a rapid tempo or with a group that's not as experienced at melismatic singing, you can trim off the alto's and baritone's last three eighth notes in measure 4, 8, and 12, holding them on a half note with the soprano.

Hanukkah Song: If you'd like a longer version, consider repeating the whole song two or three times, increasing speed with each pass.

Here We Come A-Caroling: Don't let the second half of the song slow down at all; even though the meter changes, the overall feel should remain a lilting two.

Jingle Bells: Be sure the relative volume levels allow the melodic line to be heard clearly (first the women, then the baritone, then the women, and so on). If you'd like a little percussion, you can always fall back on the old holiday trick and have folks shake their keys.

Jolly Old Saint Nicholas: Have everyone breathe at each semicolon, which will insure that the sound is unbroken through each verse as the alto carries through when the soprano and bass breathe.

O Christmas Tree: As an introduction, consider singing one verse entirely on "loo" (*a la* the Charlie Brown Christmas special).

Silent Night/Stille Nacht: Feel free to mix English and German verses to your liking (we split languages for legibility).

We Wish You a Merry Christmas: Be sure the alto countermelody is clearly heard between the soprano and bass.

- The **Definitive A Cappella Press Kit**, a guide for groups putting together their own promotional material
- **Producing the Ultimate A Cappella Show**, a how-to manual covering everything from single-group concerts to festivals
- **Starting an A Cappella Group**, a basic guide to starting up your own group for fun or profit

TO JOIN, send a check to:

CASA
2525 Van Ness Ave, Suite 205
San Francisco, CA 94109
USA

For more information, drop us a line:

Phone: 1.415.563.5224
Fax: 1.415.921.2834
Email: casa@casa.org
World Wide Web: http://www.casa.org/

TOTAL VOCAL
perfect harmony, one note at a time

Total Vocal is a company specializing in a cappella and vocal services, including:

- **Arranging**: We can provide your group with custom arrangements, published sheet music, and arranging advice. We're responsible for over 1,000 vocal arrangements in a wide array of voicings and styles, for high school, collegiate, professional and recreational groups.

> *"A battery of sounds that make mincemeat of the traditional limits of the human voice"*
> – The *Oakland Tribune*

> *"You're going to have a serious impact on the future of choral music."*
> – Kirby Shaw

- **Producing**: We can help you produce a great album, from planning and preproduction to recording, mixing and distribution. Our clients range from classical to doo-wop to pop, from high school to cutting-edge professionals.

> *"The best pure quality a cappella recording I've ever heard."*
> – Elie Landau, *Recorded A Cappella Review Board*

> *"Stellar Production Work"*
> –Mainely A Cappella

- **Directing**: We can help you form an a cappella group or other vocal music project, direct it through the initial start-up phase, and provide music direction on an ongoing basis.

> *"Soulful melodies, crashing drums, driving bass: you won't believe your ears."*
> – The New York Times

> *"Sensational Sounds! You give a whole new meaning to the word 'acappella'."*
> – Ed McMahon

- **Teaching**: We provide a number of educational services for individuals and groups on a one-time or ongoing basis, including workshops, informational booklets, group coaching and private lessons.

> *"Nothing short of wonderful; just the right mix of expertise, experience, communication skills and charisma"*
> – Colorado Vocal Jazz Society

> *"Il maestro di a cappella populare"*
> – Daigo Music School, Italy

For more information, contact:

Deke Sharon, President
Total Vocal
681 10th Avenue
San Francisco, CA 94118
Phone: 1.415.846.4073
Email: info@totalvocal.com
URL: http://www.totalvocal.com/

Other A Cappella Resources

MAINELY A CAPPELLA (MAC)
MAC is a mail-order catalog published annually with quarterly updates. It features more than 2,000 titles, including rare and international releases. The catalog represents a wide range of styles and genres - from the latest in pop, jazz and world bands to classical ensembles and barbershop harmonies.

MAC Yak
Mainely A CAPPELLA'S electronic newsletter features new releases, pre-releases, and is the only place to find great sale items.

VARSITY VOCALS
Varsity Vocals is a student a cappella outreach organization that sponsors four great programs:

The *Best of College A Cappella (BOCA)* annual compilation CD encourages college groups to compete for a place on this sought-after CD.

The *International Championship of Collegiate A Cappella (ICCA)* brings together hundreds of college a cappella singers who compete in regional concerts across North America for a place in the national finals, held in the Avery Fisher Hall of Lincoln Center, New York City.

The *Best of High School A Cappella (BOHSA)* compilation CD features high school groups from all over the world.

The *Varisty Vocals Scholarship* is a separate non-profit fund that recognizes college students who are advancing the growth of *a cappella*.

For more details see: *www.varsityvocals.com*

ON-LINE COMMUNITY
The Mainely A CAPPELLA catalog has a popular home page on the World Wide Web, at *www.a–cappella.com*. There are more than 10,000 RealAudio® and MP3 sound clips to hear, an extensive and continually updated concert calendar, and secure on-line buying. There is also a very active newsgroup on the Internet designed exclusively for a cappella fans: *rec.music.a–cappella* (on the web at *groups.google.com*).

For more information contact us:

PO Box 159
Southwest Harbor, ME 04679
Phone: 1.800.827.2936
International: 1.207.244.7603
Fax: 1.207.244.7613
Email: catalog@a-cappella.com
World Wide Web: www.a-cappella.com
For a FREE catalog call: 1.800.827.2936

Other Titles Available from
Contemporary A Cappella Publishing

Contemporary A Cappella Publishing (CAP) produces the Contemporary A Cappella Songbook Collection:

SATB Series
Volume 1	HL08741649 *
Volume 2	HL08741650 *
A CASA Christmas	HL08741651 *
Songs for All Occasions	HL08742050
I Feel Good	HL08742598 *
Shout	HL08743512
Love Songs A Cappella	HL08743515

SSAA Series
Natural Woman	HL08742904
Girls Just Want to Have Fun	*coming in 2004*
Respect	*coming in 2004*

TTBB Series
Good Ol' A Cappella	HL08743513
Sh-Boom	HL08743514

SAB Series
Under the Boardwalk	*coming in 2004*
Deck the Hall	*coming in 2004*

Jazz Series
Standards	HL08743235
Classics	*coming in 2004*

Performer Series
Continuum: The First Songbook of Sweet Honey in the Rock	HL08742029
Ticket to Ride: The Swingle Singers	HL08743854

These, in addition to *The Collegiate A Cappella Arranging Manual* (HL0874259), are available wherever songbooks are sold, or online at *www.a-cappella.com* and *www.casa.org*.

Contemporary A Cappella Publishing, Inc.
P.O. Box 159 · Southwest Harbour, ME 04679
www.capublish.com

* Part-predominant learning tapes and CDs are available for the arrangements in these volumes directly from Mainely A CAPPELLA. Call 1.800.827.2936, email *order@a-cappella.com* or order online at *www.a-cappella.com* and specify Soprano, Alto, Tenor, Bass, or a set of all four.